INTRODUCTION

What do Buddha, Plato, Sukune of ancient Japan, the Bible's Jacob, Henry the Eighth, Abe Lincoln, and Leo Tolstoy have in common? Since this is a book about wrestling, the answer should be obvious: they practiced wrestling, one of the world's oldest and most popular sports.

Although the birth of the sport is obscured in prehistory and legends, we do have evidence of its existence in the form of French cave paintings and 4000-year-old Egyptian hieroglyphics. The wrestlers carved in stone deep in the ancient tomb of Ben Hasan can be seen using holds that are amazingly similar to those used today.

The Greeks were very enthusiastic about wrestling and made it the deciding event of the early Olympic Games. Their versions resembled our freestyle and Greco-Roman wrestling, although they were somewhat violent for modern taste—it wasn't unusual for contestants to have their teeth knocked out.

Wrestling thrived through the ages and people of every region developed their own variations—Sumo in Japan, Koshti in Turkey, Glima in Iceland. Modern wrestling really began in 1896 as an Olympic sport, when five competitors entered a Greco-Roman wrestling event. Greco-Roman wrestling is a variant style that was developed in France and was popular during the 19th century. It still is popular in Europe today. Freestyle was added to the Olympics at the St. Louis games in 1904, and since then wrestling has been growing in popularity in this country. Greco-Roman wrestling is basically the same as freestyle wrestling but only allows the wrestler to use the upper body to grasp the opponent's upper body. It is much more popular outside the United States.

The first organized wrestling meet in the U.S. took place around the turn of the century, and in 1903 the first college wrestling conference was formed. As the sport's popularity grew, other conferences came into existence. In the United States today there are four major amateur wrestling organizations: USA Wrestling, the AAU (Amateur Athletic Union), NHSAA (National Federation of State High School Athletic Associations), and the NCAA (National College Athletic Association). USA Wrestling and the AAU adhere to the rules as set forth by FILA (Federation Internationale de Lutte Amateur), the sport's international governing body. USA Wrestling and AAU rules differ slightly from those of NHSAA, which governs high school athletics, and the NCAA. NHSAA and NCAA rule codes are similar and have evolved over the last ninety years to suit student athletes and administrations.

This book explains the rules for international wrestling style based on the AAU's rules. The reason these rules were chosen is that they are used worldwide, from Turkey, to Japan, to Peru, for all international competition and the Olympics. When a group travels abroad to wrestle or a foreign group visits the U.S., these are the rules participants must adhere to.

The differences between the rules set forth by the AAU and those of the NHSAA and the NCAA are not that great. For instance, high school wrestlers are required to wear ear guards—others are not. But there are some other more important differences. The international rules allow a full nelson to the head (from the side), while the NCAA and NHSAA do not. Collegiate wrestlers may use a "figure 4" hold on the head of an opponent; international competitors may not. Collegiate wrestlers get points for riding time (simply holding an opponent) or for escaping a hold. In international wrestling, there are no points awarded for riding time, and a full reversal—not just an escape—must be achieved for points to be awarded, rather than just an escape. Points for back exposure are awarded much more quickly under international rules. In general, the AAU rules make the wrestling more exciting to watch and reward the wrestler who takes the initiative rather than the one who reacts.

Spurred along by the formation of clubs on the youth level and the exposure that the sport has received through the Olympic Games, wrestling has grown tremendously over the last two decades. Conservatively estimated, a quarter of a million people participate in amateur wrestling in the U.S. through USA Wrestling or the AAU. The majority of high schools and a great many colleges have now included wrestling in their physical education programs. Why is wrestling so popular today?

One reason is that wrestlers find the one-on-one challenge very emotionally satisfying and, like most sports, it demands and fosters real athletic ability and self-discipline. In particular, wrestling causes an overall balanced development of the body and brings into play the strength and flexibility of every muscle group. And while it may look to a casual observer to be nothing more than violent hand-to-hand combat, wrestling's rules and requirements and prohibitions, combined with the intense involvement of the officials, add up to something much more than that. It is a test of strength and skill between two opponents, a contest not to see who can hurt the other, but of who is stronger and can dominate by skill, intelligence, and strength. While the wrestlers struggle toward the ultimate goal—holding the opponent's shoulders to the mat for an instant—the official watches carefully and along the way awards them points for skill.

Not only is the sport good for the body, it is accessible. Any reasonably fit competitor, regardless of height or weight, can participate with an equal chance of achieving success. This healthful sport rewards hard work, is wonderfully economical, and does not require an expensive facility or equipment.

I hope this book will be useful and will help clear up confusion for the beginning wrestler or spectator and increase the overall enjoyment of the sport itself.

AMATEUR WRESTLING
RULES IN PICTURES

Michael Brown

Book Consultant: Special Thanks to Larry Bergstrom,
Treasurer of the Amateur Athletic Union, National Wrestling Committee

A Perigee Book

Perigee Books
are published by
The Putnam Publishing Group
200 Madison Avenue
New York, NY 10016

The rules depicted herein are those of the Amateur Athletic Union and may differ slightly from those of the National Federation of State High School Athletic Associations, USA Wrestling, and the National College Athletic Association. The AAU adheres to the rules set forth by FILA (Federation Internationale de Lutte Amateur).

Library of Congress Cataloging-in-Publication Data

Brown, Michael, date.
    Amateur wrestling rules in pictures / Michael Brown; book consultant, Larry Bergstrom.
        p.   cm.
    price.
    1. Wrestling—Rules.   2. Wrestling—Rules—Pictorial works.
    I. Bergstrom, Larry.   II. Title.
    GV1196.27.B76   1989   89-36863 CIP
    796.8′12—dc20
ISBN 0-399-51589-5

Printed in the United States of America
1 2 3 4 5 6 7 8 9 10

EQUIPMENT AND STAFF

Preparations are being made for an important wrestling tournament. The bouts haven't begun yet, but there's a lot of activity going on. Officials in uniform check the equipment and confer as they move around the floor. People are setting up tables and chairs, taping mats, and tacking signs to the walls. This isn't aimless activity. The equipment is being arranged and the tournament is organized to ensure fairness, safety, and the maximum of wrestling action. Let's examine some of the most important points.

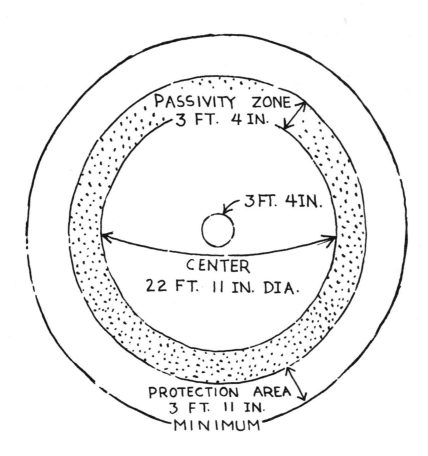

THE MAT

The requirements for the size of the mats vary slightly according to what sort of tournament is being held. The main point of these rules is not to make participants rush around with rulers, but to make sure that the mats will be big and safe enough for wrestling. In general, the measurements described in the diagram are required for major national and international events. For lesser events slightly smaller mats can be used. Mats should be 1.5 to 2.5 inches thick and covered in a material that can be cleaned and disinfected.

Mats are divided into three areas. The innermost portion is called the center; the red ring surrounding the center is the passivity zone; and the outer ring is the protection area. These zones don't function like the lines on a basketball court, where a touch of the line means an immediate stop of play. They are more like guideposts for the sake of safety and to compel the wrestlers to confront one another. The mats should be raised if spectators can't see well, and they should be set up in an open space so that the officials can do their jobs.

OFFICIALS

In general, bouts should have four officials: one referee, one judge, a mat chairman, and one controller. In AAU youth competition, this requirement is flexible. Officials should wear white.

COACHES

During the match, coaches must not stand on the platform if the mat is raised, or stand any closer than 13 feet from the edge of the mat if it's not raised. Coaches aren't allowed to insult the judges or referees or try to affect the bout. If they do any of these things, the referees will give them a yellow-card warning. If they continue to misbehave, they'll get a red-card elimination and must leave the tournament. In other words, they can only give instructions during the rest period. Another rule for coaches in AAU wrestling is that they must wear a team warm-up suit or civilian clothes.

MEDICAL ATTENDANTS

Whoever organizes the tournament is supposed to provide qualified medical attendants to oversee the weigh-in, the bouts, and detect possible drug use.

THE WRESTLERS

Opening ceremonies are over and the wrestlers are getting set to begin. At some point before their first bout, all of them will stretch out their muscles and warm up. Some psych themselves up while others get last-minute instructions from their coaches. As they adjust their equipment, a few team members chat with each other and try to stay relaxed. It's not easy to keep from having butterflies. They've worked hard to get ready for today and doing well in the tournament means a lot to them. Let's take a closer look at these participants.

Correct wrestling uniform and acceptable knee pads

This type of bandage and splint are definitely not acceptable

DRESS

Wrestlers should come to the mat wearing a single-piece outfit, known as a singlet, in the color—always red or blue—assigned to them for that match. The outfit should be snug, cover the body starting at mid-thigh, and have the right size arm and neck openings. They may use knee pads if they like, but wrestlers aren't allowed to wear any other kind of wrap or supporting bandages that might prevent proper holds. They may bandage slight injuries or scrapes. Shoes should be lightweight and cover the ankle. They may not have any kind of spikes, buckles, metal parts, or hard soles. Wrestlers should never grease themselves or arrive for the match already sweaty, and they must carry a handkerchief. They may not wear any object that could hurt the other wrestler. At weigh-in the wrestlers must either be clean shaven or have a well-established beard. In other words, they can't be wearing just enough whiskers to make their faces feel like sandpaper.

WEIGH-IN

Officially designated doctors will examine competitors just prior to weigh-in, which will be overseen by tournament officials. The doctors will be looking for any indication of contagious disease and they'll also make sure the wrestlers' fingernails are short. For tournaments that last more than one day, competitors are weighed in each day.

WEIGHT CLASSES—AGE CATEGORIES

AAU and USA Wrestling and the other organizations' weight classes vary slightly. Contestants may enter an event in only one weight class, either the one they match at weigh-in, or the one immediately above their actual weight.

Age category is determined by the participant's year of birth. It doesn't matter whether you were born on January 1 or December 31 of that year—that is your age category.

Nevertheless, your age category won't really matter if you don't have a valid proof of registration. It's required and you have to bring it to weigh-in. And don't forget, drug use also is formally forbidden.

THE BOUT

The bouts, the basic units of wrestling, have begun and in each one the wrestlers are going at it one to one. The gym is filled with the sound of wrestlers crashing to the mat, whistles, and shouts. Some bouts seem to end when they have barely begun, while others seem to go on in a continuous series of TAKEDOWNS and TIE-UPS and ESCAPES. Other bouts start, stop, start, then stop again. The referee will try to allow safe and continuous wrestling to go on so that scoring can be achieved. The wrestlers will be warned if they are straying and should try to move themselves back to the center. If there is a pause in the action and the wrestlers have jockeyed or rolled too far, or if they are in danger of leaving the mat altogether, the referee will give them a fresh start in the center. Understanding why decisions are made to stop and restart the bout is not as difficult as it may seem. Keep in mind the goal of safe and continuous wrestling, and understand the function of the mat's three zones, and it will make sense.

CALL TO MAT

When it's their turn to compete, wrestlers will be called to the mat in a loud, clear voice. If they don't arrive promptly, they will lose the bout. A delay of up to three minutes is okay in the first bout in the first round, but the tardy wrestler must have an acceptable reason.

START

When a wrestler's name is called, the wrestler should go to the area that is the appropriate color—i.e., the same color the wrestler is wearing. The referee, standing in the center of the mat, calls both wrestlers forward, shakes their hands, inspects their uniforms and their skin for lubrications or sweat, looks at their hands and fingernails, and makes sure each has a handkerchief. When the referee is satisfied, the wrestlers greet one another, shake hands, and return to their corners. The ref blows the whistle and the wrestlers approach each other and start wrestling. No more handshaking until the bout's over.

DURATION

Older wrestlers have one 5-minute period for wrestling, while younger wrestlers' bouts are broken by a short rest period.

REST

During the rest period the coach may come to the edge of the mat and attend to the wrestler.

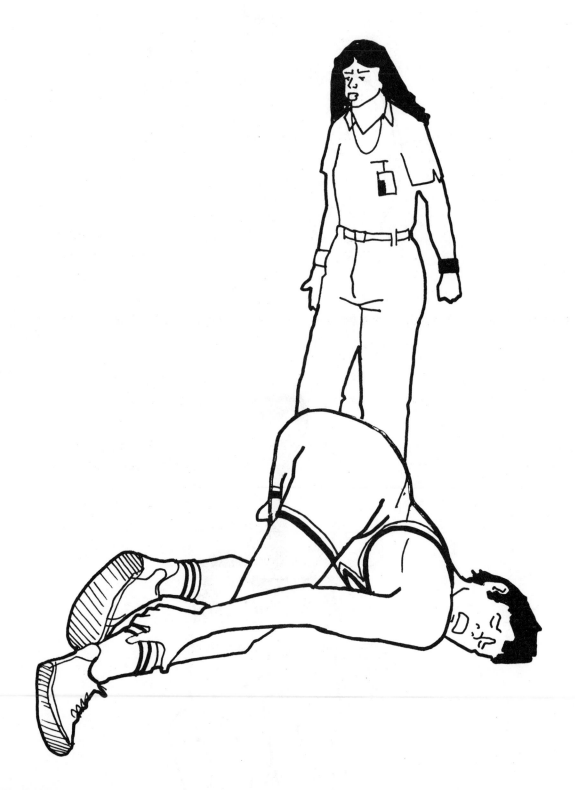

TIME-OUTS

If a wrestler needs to stop because of a nosebleed, a fall to the head, or another legitimate reason, including problems with contact lenses or equipment, the referee can halt the bout. A wrestler may need several injury time-outs, but should be brief about it, because using more than two minutes for injury during one match will cause the bout to end and the wrestler with the problem to lose. That wrestler and coach will be advised minute by minute of the time. At the end of two minutes, a medical attendant will say whether the bout can continue.

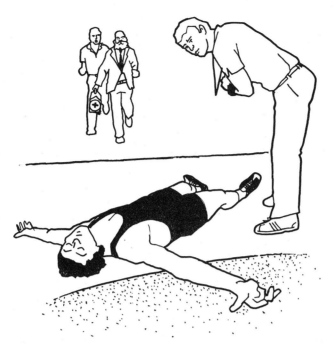

INTERVENTION BY DOCTOR

The medical attendants mentioned earlier may stop a bout whenever they think a competitor is in danger. They should ask the mat chairman to stop the action, and they may end the match by declaring that one wrestler is unfit to continue.

Mat chairmen can also interrupt bouts if the judge or referee makes a serious mistake. Chairman, judge, and ref will confer and start the bout again when they have settled the matter. Contestants may not interrupt the bout themselves.

Neither coaches nor contestants may interrupt a bout themselves, and they certainly may not decide when the opponents are to stop and return to the middle of the mat.

OUT-OF-BOUNDS

One of the most common reasons that a bout may be stopped is if the wrestlers move out-of-bounds. The criteria for out-of-bounds vary from situation to situation.

In cases of *standing wrestling*, the referee will stop the bout and the wrestlers will go back and resume wrestling in the middle of the mat if:
— one wrestler's foot touches the protection area or if the move ends in the protection area, or
— a move in the passivity zone is not executed in a continuous manner.

The referee will also stop the bout and send the wrestlers back to the center if wrestlers in a tie-up or in open stances enter the zone within three or four feet without executing the hold. They'll also stop the bout if the wrestlers completely leave the mat.

If *wrestling occurs on the ground*, the bout will be stopped and the wrestlers will go back and resume wrestling standing in the middle of the mat if there is a stalemate in the wrestling without holds or moves.

The bout is also stopped in cases of a hold begun on the ground and ending in the protection area. Or when a wrestler whose back is in danger slides from the mat to the protection area or touches the protection area with a shoulder or neck. This wrestler probably will be called out. However the call would depend on the reaction of the wrestlers, whether or not they are moving toward the center of the mat. The officials will allow the attacking wrestler time to move the opponent back to the center of the mat.

The bout is also stopped if a wrestler, while under control, touches the protection area with the head while flat on the back on the mat. Note that ground wrestling will be used to restart the bout in the center only when the attacked wrestler was truly being dominated by the opponent.

GROUND WRESTLING

When ground wrestling has been specified, the competitors take these positions: BOTTOM: The attacked wrestler kneels and places both hands on the mat, hands and elbows apart, eight inches from the knees. TOP: The dominant wrestler must first contact the attacked wrestler on flat of his back with both hands parallel. Then, when the referee whistles the match to begin, the wrestler on top may go into any position desired, as pictured above. The referee will send the wrestlers back to the center and require the action to resume with ground wrestling when: The attacked is truly dominated by the opponent; the two go out-of-bounds through the zone and onto the protection area; and the attacked wrestler, under control, touches the protection area with the head while flat on the back on the mat.

ENDING

The timekeeper rings a bell or uses some other appropriate device to indicate the end of a period or bout. At once the referee blows the whistle. After a rest period, the bout continues with both wrestlers standing, no matter what position they were in at the end of the period.

END OF THE BOUT

The bout is finished. The loser congratulates the winner, who thanks the loser and shakes a few hands. Now it's time to get ready for the next bout. There's little time to think back over the countless varieties of holds that might have been used or the numberless tactical twists that might have been tried. The wrestlers' names will be called again and within a few minutes they will be back on the mat wrestling different opponents.

Here's what ends a bout:
- A fall or technical superiority is established.
  Remember, it takes two officials confirming a fall for a fall to be called.
- One of the wrestlers is disqualified or eliminated.
- There is an injury.
- The time expires.

If time expires, the wrestlers shake hands and wait by the referee for the decision. When the decision is made, the winner's arm is raised by the ref. Then the wrestlers shake hands with the ref and the opposing coach. Don't think of this as an option: a wrestler may be sanctioned for walking off in a gloat or a sulk if he does not honor these amenities. In case of a tie, overtime is called and takes place immediately following the bout, with no rest period. The first point scored stops the bout and the wrestler who scores it wins!

THE FALL

The fall may be the most spectacular way to win a bout. A fall occurs when a wrestler holds the opponent so that both shoulders touch the mat, and holds the opponent there long enough for the referee to see that the control is total enough for a pin. The head of the controlled wrestler can't touch the protection surface.

It is vital that a fall be clearly held; the two shoulders of the downed wrestler *must* be flat against the mat long enough for the ref to make a positive determination.

TECHNICAL SUPERIORITY

If there's no fall, a wrestler may win by technical superiority. The bout will stop before the time is up when there's a difference of 15 technical points between the wrestlers. The match won't be stopped for technical superiority if there is an ongoing attack and immediate counterattack.

TIES

If the wrestlers have equal points at the end of the time, the winner is decided in sudden-death overtime (whoever scores first wins).

ELIMINATION AND DISQUALIFICATION

Wrestlers can be eliminated for a variety of misbehaviors, which will be illustrated in detail later.

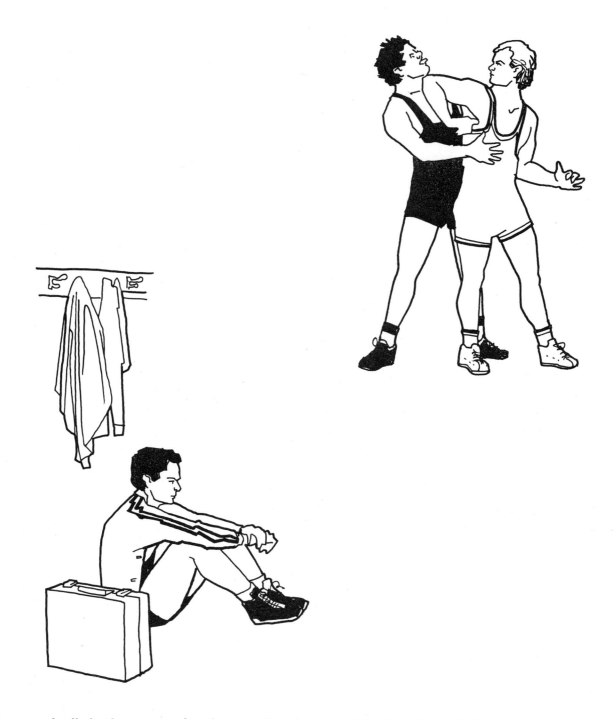

In general, elimination occurs after three cautions for passivity or infractions of other rules. The eliminated wrestler may continue to participate in the tournament. Elimination by disqualification is more serious, and has to do with foul play, cheating, or any intentional illegal action that could cause serious injury to the opponent. Wrestlers guilty of these actions will lose the bout and will not place or figure in any way in the tournament. If a wrestler picks up a second loss in the finals of the tournament and that loss is from disqualification or for passivity, the wrestler will not place in the tournament.
Wrestlers disqualified for outright brutality are utterly disqualified and do not place in the tournament.

THE GOOD STUFF

Now for the fun stuff. So far we've been looking at the nuts and bolts of a bout, the officials, equipment, what's expected of the wrestlers before they actually may begin wrestling, how the bout is started and stopped. Now it's time to talk about the essence of wrestling.

One of the most common ways to win a bout is by scoring technical points. Two main concepts to keep in mind are, first, that dropping the opponent to the mat and dominating him leads to points, and second, that new situations must develop and new challenges be met before more points may be scored.

And remember that good wrestling is not the only way to score technical points. Points are also awarded to a wrestler as a means of penalizing the opponent. One or two points may be awarded the wrestler whose opponent does something illegal. But we'll explore this later.

Don't be confused by the other kinds of points that are used to conduct a tournament. There are positive points that help to determine a wrestler's status in the elimination round of a tournament. The higher the quality of the win, the more positive points are awarded. There are also team points awarded to a wrestling team for their top-two winners in each weight category, which helps determine team champs at the end of the tournament.

SCORES FOR MOVES

The referee, mat judge, and mat chair score the bout as it is being wrestled.

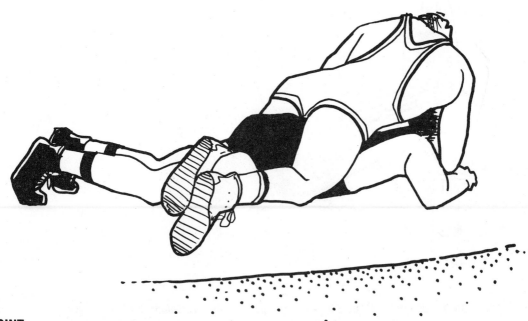

ONE POINT
Here's how one point is scored:
— The attacking wrestler brings the opponent down to the mat, goes behind, holds down and controls the opponent with three points of contact—two arms and one knee, or two knees and one arm, as pictured.
— A wrestler executes a proper hold for standing or ground wrestling without placing the opponent in danger of a fall.
— A wrestler escapes, goes behind and holds and controls the opponent.

The wrestler forces the opponent back on one or two arms and the opponent's back is exposed, but not touching the mat. More on back exposure later. (See page 36 for more on back exposure.)

A wrestler earns a point if he legally blocks a hold.

A wrestler earns a point if the opponent flees the mat.

TWO POINTS
In ground wrestling back exposure generally scores two points.

Here, the wrestler executes a good hold on the ground, making the opponent's back briefly touch the mat, placing the opponent in a touch fall.

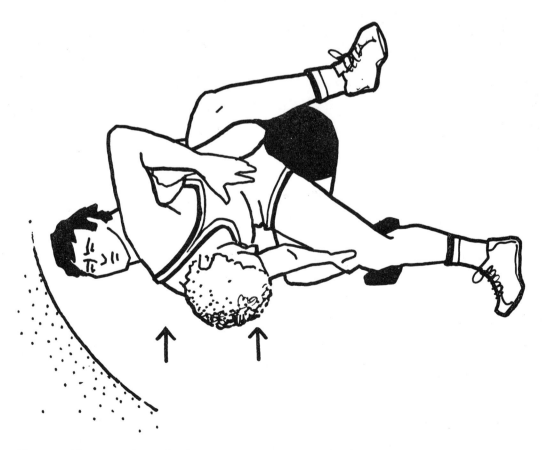

Two points: The attacking wrestler rolls the opponent across the shoulders.

Two points: The attacking wrestler scores because the opponent flees a hold and leaves the wrestling area touching both shoulders to the mat.

The attacked wrestler scores two points because the attacker has landed on both shoulders or rolled across the shoulders while attempting a hold.

Attacked wrestlers score two points by blocking the attackers who have their back in contact with the mat.

Any wrestler scores two points by completing a GRAND TECHNIQUE without directly and immediately touching the opponent's back to danger. An explanation of this will follow shortly.

The attacking wrestler scores two points if the opponent uses an illegal hold to block a move.

THREE POINTS
A wrestler scores three points for executing a standing throw of modest proportion that puts the opponent's back in danger.

The wrestler scores three points when the opponent is lifted from the mat with a large, full throw. It's okay if the attacker has one or two knees on the mat, as long as the opponent's back is immediately placed in danger. It still counts as a major throw.

FIVE POINTS

Grand technique is certainly grand, but it is rare. To merit this title the move or hold must do all these things:

- — force the opponent to leave the ground completely;
- — control the opponent;
- — propel the opponent through the air in a large, full curve; and
- — return the opponent to the ground directly into a position of immediate danger.

BACK EXPOSURE

Many of the moves leading to the scores listed above depend on the attacking wrestler putting the opponent in back danger. Wrestlers reach a "position of danger" if the line of their backs forms less-than-90-degree angles, vertically or parallel, to the mat, and the wrestler accordingly resists the "fall" with the upper body. A wrestler may resist with head, elbows, or shoulders.

BACK EXPOSURE
Back exposure caused by the defensive wrestler bridging to avoid a fall.

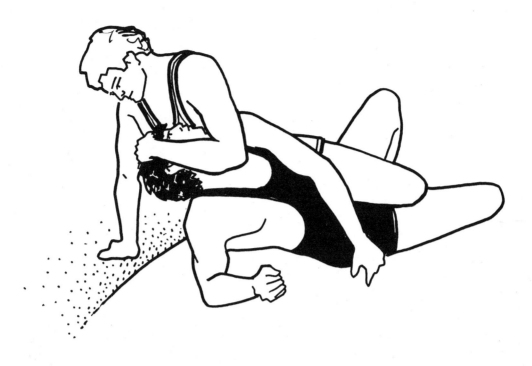

Back exposure occurring when the defense wrestler, while attempting to avoid touching the shoulders to the mat, is pressed against an elbow or both elbows with back exposed.

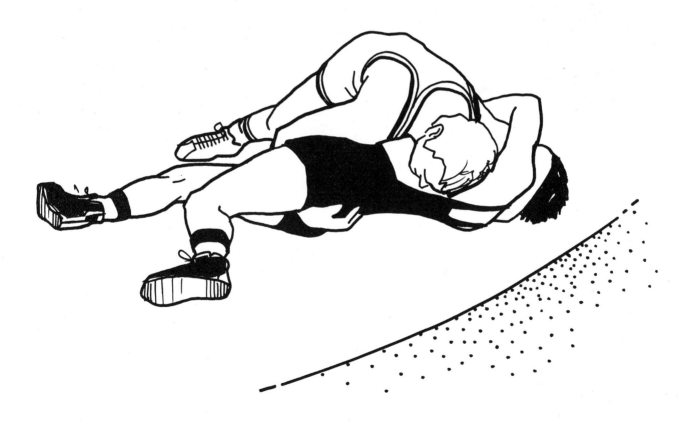

Here, back exposure exists because the wrestler with one shoulder in contact with the mat is breaking the vertical line of 90 degrees with the other shoulder.

Here, back exposure exists because the wrestler's two shoulders have touched briefly.

The wrestler rolls across both shoulders, causing back exposure to exist.

Back exposure exists because the wrestler escapes, but then exposes the back. In this illustration, if the escaping wrestler caused the escape and the attacking wrestler did not follow with control, the escaping wrestler would not lose any points.

The **GUT WRENCH** is one way to bring about back exposure, but keep in mind that an attacking wrestler cannot make consecutive scores with a gut wrench or variations. Once the gut wrench was completed, it would be easy for the wrestler to win by repeating the move over and over. For every point scored by use of a gut wrench, the attacker has to do something a little more interesting for the next point. Remember, a move scores at the end of the period if it was completed before the bell.

GENERAL PROHIBITIONS

Wrestling is one of the oldest sports in existence, more ancient than the written word. Small wonder, then, that wrestlers are sometimes possessed by primitive impulses. A good number of the rules in this section cover things that the wrestlers might find themselves doing and then feeling very apologetic about afterwards.

Don't pull hair!

No biting any part of the body . . .

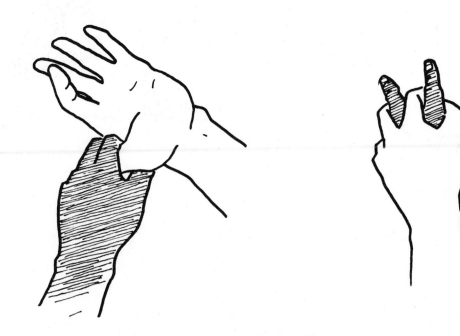

. . . and no pulling and twisting the fingers.

This isn't boxing—no punching allowed.

Leave the butting to the billy goats . . .

. . . and the kicking to the mules.

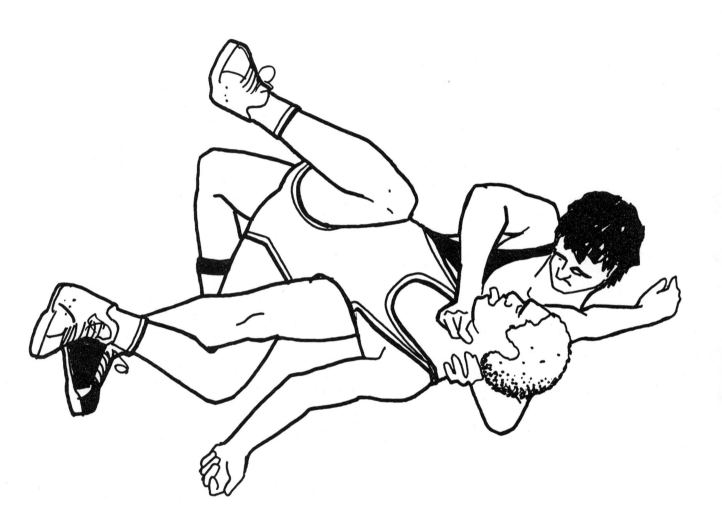

No strangling or choking.

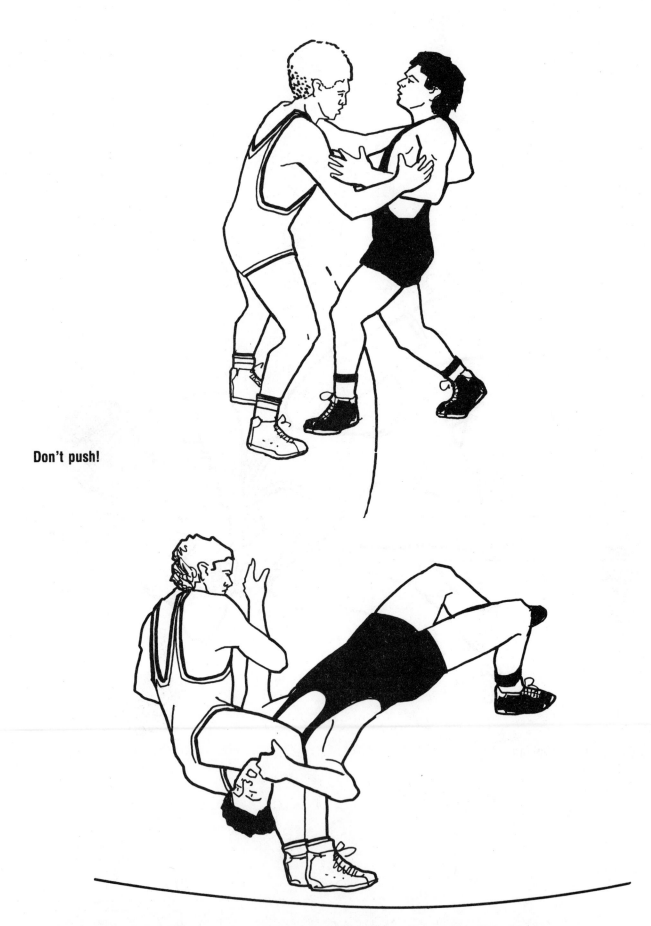

Don't push!

Don't make moves or holds with the intention of hurting opponents to the point that they must quit. Don't do things that may endanger lives or fracture or dislocate opponents' limbs. In short, don't try to maim and kill.

Walk on your own feet, not your opponent's.

Don't touch their faces between eyebrow and mouth.

Don't force your elbows or knees into the opponent's chest or stomach.

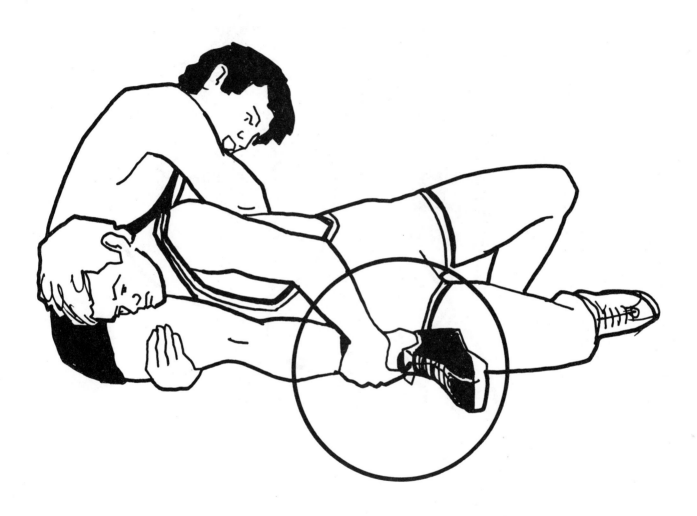

Don't twist in a way that could injure the opponent.

Wrestle with the opponent, not the opponent's singlet.

Don't grab or cling to the mat . . .

. . . and don't speak to the opponents at all, not to comment on the smell of their cologne and not to express what you think of the wrestler's family members.

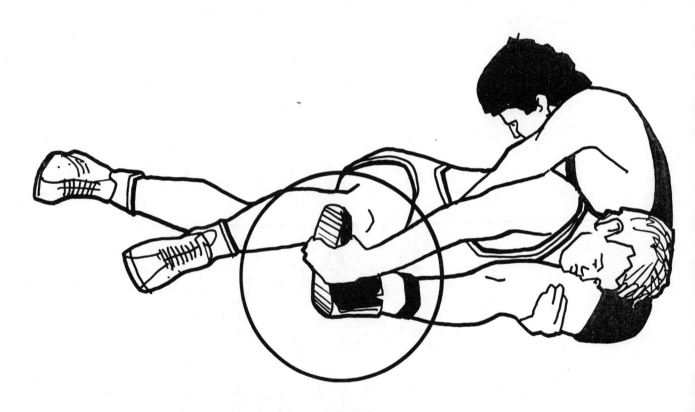

Don't grab the opponent by the soles of the feet—only above the foot or by the heel is permitted.

ILLEGAL HOLDS

The medical personnel and mat chairman are up from their seats. A wrestler has been injured and they're calling the doctor over the P.A. system. The wrestler is still on the mat, injured by an illegal hold. Now, instead of the enjoyment of skill and competition, we have pain, dark looks, disappointment, and remorse.

The rules in this section are the most important in the sport. They exist solely to safeguard the wrestler's safety. Although there may seem to be a confusing variety of illegal holds, it's not really hard to understand how they work. Human joints are not made of rubber— they only bend in certain ways. Almost all these holds are illegal because when they are undertaken, a wrestler's joints may be twisted the wrong way, causing severe pain and injury.

ILLEGAL HOLDS

Aaack! Not by the throat!

You may not bend the opponent's arms behind the back more than 90 degrees.

Don't use both hands to get the opponent in a headlock on the neck.

You may not grab your opponent by the forearms and force the arms above the head.

A FULL NELSON is an expression that is familiar to almost everyone, even if they don't know what it means. Its definition in wrestling is: to encircle the opponent under the arms and behind the neck, as shown here. To apply leverage in this position could cripple the attacked wrestler.

Don't do this: grab the opponent's arm behind the back from above and press it so that the forearm and upper arm are angled at less than a 90-degree angle. Known as the **CHICKEN WING**, it's not allowed.

Leave this sort of manuever to the chiropractor. Specifically, don't execute a hold that stretches the opponent's backbone.

A wrestler should not hold the opponent in a head-only headlock with arms and hands locked.

This is a legal headlock.

Never, when holding your opponent upside down, drive his body straight down into the earth as if driving a post-hole digger. Do it sideways. In Greco-Roman style, some part of the attacker's body (besides the feet) must reach the mat before the upper part of the opponent's body.

Don't pick opponents up from a bridge and throw them back on the mat.

In a similar vein, don't drive an opponent forward out of a bridge.

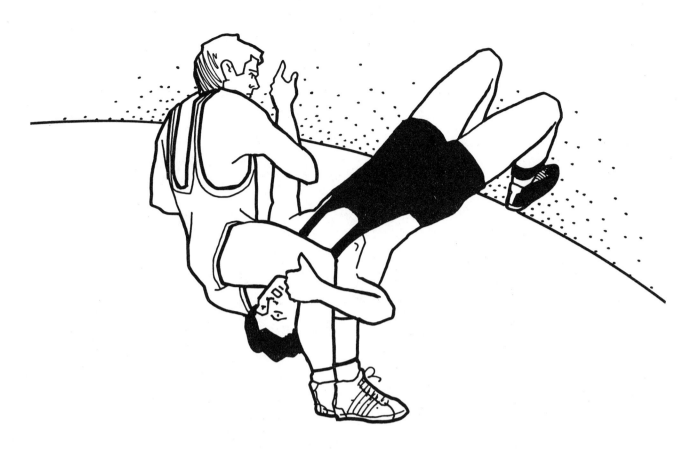

It's not allowed to use **LEG SCISSORS** on the neck, head, or body, just on the legs or arms.

In fact, no type of **SCISSOR LOCK** is permitted on the neck, head, or body.

Greco-Roman wrestling is a form of wrestling more popular in Europe than in the U.S. It is similar in many ways to the more familiar freestyle wrestling, but does not allow attacks on the opponent's legs or the use of legs in holds.

If your opponent is taken down, you must move with him to the mat.

CONSEQUENCES OF ILLEGAL HOLDS

The referee's priorities, when an infraction is committed, go something like this:
— stop the infraction
— break the hold, if it's dangerous
— caution
— declare that the wrestler is at fault, or has lost, or is disqualified, and
— award points

The referee will interfere as little as possible while still insuring that the wrestling proceeds swiftly and safely. Nevertheless, it's the ref's responsibility to stimulate solid, worthwhile wrestling and referees can choose different ways to modify and compel the action. They can do this by halting a bout and commenting on ineffective wrestling and encourage the practice of genuine wrestling. A good ref can distinguish easily between a dominated wrestler and one that's passive. This ref will not hesitate to make calls on passivity, but won't disqualify wrestlers who, though being controlled, are trying hard.

When a wrestler does commit illegal moves, there will be unpleasant consequences. Specifically:

—If a wrestler put himself at a disadvantage by applying an illegal hold, that wrestler is out of luck. The bout will continue, and when the point is scored the offending wrestler will receive a caution and the opponent an extra point.

—If a wrestler applies an illegal hold, any advantage gained will be voided, the wrestler will be cautioned, and the opponent will receive a point.

—Using an illegal hold to keep an opponent from developing a hold will cost the offender a caution and give the opponent one or two points.

—A referee should try to stop violations without breaking the hold. If the offended wrestler is not in too much danger, the ref might allow the hold to continue, and once the move is completed either accept the hold or void it and caution the offending wrestler.

—If a legal hold becomes illegal, points are awarded up to the point where the hold went bad.

—If the offense is willful head butting or any other brutality, the offender can be disqualified.

PASSIVITY

What a bout! Two wrestlers, old opponents, old friends, and they are really going at it. One's strong, but the other one is quicker, and both want to see who's worked harder since last time. After the bout, they'll be slapping each other on the back, trading wrestling secrets, and laughing. But they came to wrestle, both respect the sport, and neither would think of manipulating the rules in order to stall their way to victory.

Wrestlers might try to "dive out-of-bounds" to save themselves from a fall. Near the end of the bout, they might tie up the arms of their opponent, not even trying for a takedown, hoping to preserve a slim lead. These and other dull forms of rule manipulation are what the passivity laws are aimed at preventing. It's not easy to call passivity violations, especially near the end of a bout when it might make the difference between winning and losing.

PASSIVITY

This wrestler is guilty of passivity because he has intentionally fled the mat. He'd be equally guilty if he'd done it while standing.

The wrestler lying down is not trying to execute a real hold—that's passivity.

Both of these are guilty. The one on the right is pushing the opponent out, and the one at left is obstructing proper holds. This is not a common situation, but it does occur.

These wrestlers are moving toward the protection area, but they are trying to wrestle and are not being passive.

PASSIVITY ON GROUND

Becoming a human lump, that is to say, lying flat on the chest in a closed position, is definitely passive.

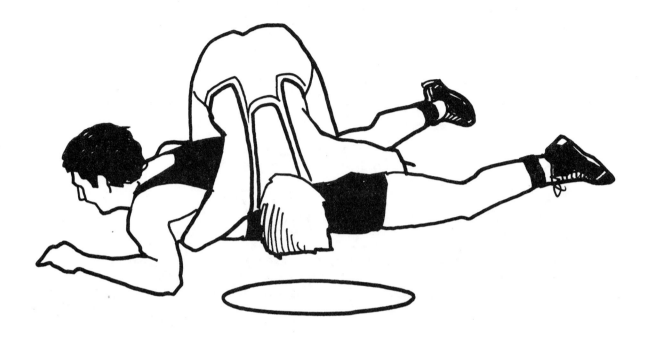

PENALTIES AND CAUTIONS

Technical points are not subtracted from a wrestler's score if that wrestler is cautioned for passivity. Cautions for illegal holds that don't affect the action cost the offender one point. If they do affect action they'll cost two points.

The ref's job isn't just to punish and award; he may also make remarks to a faulting wrestler without actually calling an offense. Although a referee might feel like suggesting, ''Do something, you lazy slugs!'' a more gentlemanly ''Action, please'' is more likely.

A wrestler who is continually passive or who makes an illegal hold after a second caution will be eliminated from the bout by a majority vote of the officials. The head official must concur.

OFFICIALS

Blowing whistles, ringing bells, slapping the mat, shouting—the guys in the white suits sure seem to make a commotion. Some sit still while others are always moving, sitting down, standing up, crouching, waving hands. In truth, an official's idea of a great job would probably be to go almost entirely unnoticed. When things are going well, the ref interferes with the wrestling as little as possible.

The ideal is that the action should continue uninterrupted. Toward this end, the referee, the official closest to the action on the mat, will try to verbally, physically, or visually warn the wrestlers as soon as a dangerous hold seems to be developing, or if the wrestlers are straying toward the edge of the mat. The wrestlers will try to work with the ref, moving back to the center of the mat or changing the illegal hold before the ref is forced to blow the whistle. Referees want to avoid that, and still keep things safe and fair.

Some important things to watch for: the referee slapping the mat to signal a victory by fall; the wrestlers being officially cautioned; the mat judge signaling to the referee. Listen for the bell ending the bout and for the ref's whistle stopping and starting it for infractions and stalemates.

A large number of rules cover the conduct and duties of the officials. Everything—from what they wear to the order that hands are shaken after the bout. Let's touch on some high points.

NUMBER OF OFFICIALS

As mentioned earlier, there should be four officials at competitions, though there won't always be that many at grass-root level events. The four are: 1 referee, 1 judge, 1 mat chairman, and 1 controller.

REFEREE
The referee out on the mat runs the bout according to the rules.

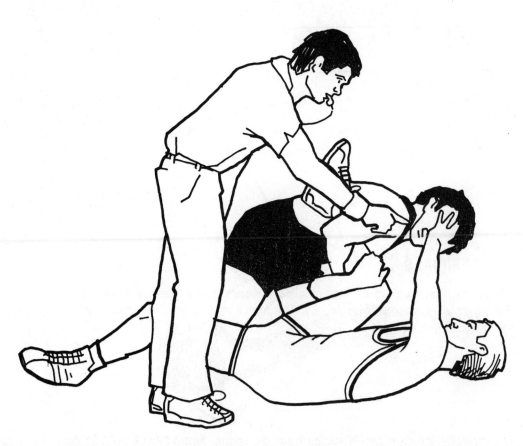

Referees are supposed to follow the movements of the wrestlers closely, but not interfere unnecessarily with their action.

Referees must wear a red band on their left wrist and a blue band on their right. After execution of a valid hold, the referee indicates the score by holding up the appropriate number of fingers with the arm that's banded in the scoring wrestler's color.

Good referees carefully monitor their distance from the action. Some moves need to be observed from a close distance; others—leg movements, for instance—are seen better from a greater distance.

JUDGE
Following each move the judge writes down the points to be scored based on the referee's score and combined with his own assessment. He'll show the score on boards placed near him. These boards should be visible to both wrestlers and spectators.

The judge can bring something to the attention of the referee if the judge disagrees with a call or thinks the ref might have missed something. The judge does this by raising the appropriately colored paddle. If judge and ref agree about a call, the decision does not include the mat chairman, except when calling a win by technical superiority.

Judges are allowed to move about, especially in close calls, but only at the edge of the mat near their station.

MAT CHAIRMAN
Though not included in every decision, this official has the final say-so. Among other things, he may halt the bout and question the decisions of the ref and judge. In score or victory disagreements between judge and referee, the mat chair provides the deciding vote.

Referee's raising the arms to signal the score and if judge and ref agree, it's official.

When there's a disagreement, the mat chair and judge counter the ref's hand signal by lifting a paddle that displays a contradictory number. The judge and chair should have paddles numbered 1, 2, 3 and 5; a white one to signal no opinion, and a red one and blue one for warnings. They may not abstain, and good officials vote clearly and leave no room for doubt. Usually the score will be determined by judge and ref and the mat chair gets involved only in disagreements, and then decides it not by calling for a new score altogether, but by siding with one of the other officials.

When the bout uses all the time allotted to it, the judge and mat chair's bout sheets decide the victor.

TOURNAMENT

It's been a great weekend of wrestling. Soon we'll see the final bouts. A few folks have departed the gym, since their favorites are out of the competition, but most have stayed. There's been a lot going on—clinics, demonstrations, old friends getting together. Parents, coaches, and fans all seem anxious to move to a spot where they can get a good look at the final bouts. We've been trying to understand the rules of wrestling by looking at the bouts and what goes on during them. They are a wrestling event's basic building blocks. Let's see how those blocks have been put together to create a tournament and select the champions.

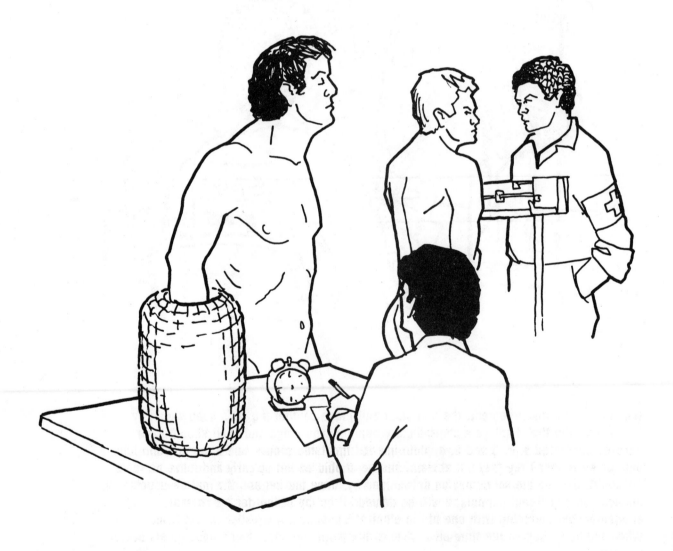

DRAWING AND POOLING

Before the tournament begins, participants in each weight and age category may be pooled into two elimination groups and then paired within these groups. This is done by drawing lots at the time of weigh-in.

PAIRING

Once all participants are paired, the pairings and timetable should be displayed where all the contestants can see them, and this schedule should be left up throughout the event. If there's an odd number of contestants, the one who drew the largest number will advance to the next round without points and will be moved to the top of the pairing chart.

The paired wrestlers will then wrestle in elimination rounds. A wrestler who is twice defeated during these rounds is out of the tournament.

ROUND-ROBIN

When the top three wrestlers in each pool are determined, round-robin competition will take place among them. A round-robin is a system whereby each wrestler in a group wrestles every other wrestler in that group. Their standing in the pool—first, second, or third—will be determined by the points they are awarded at the end of their bouts. Not all victories are awarded the same number of points. For example:

Winner, 4 Loser, 0	for a fall, technical superiority with a 15-point margin, injury, withdrawal, forfeit, failure to appear, disqualification for unsporting behavior
Winner, 3.5 Loser, 0	when the bout ends with a difference of 12 to 14 points and the loser has no technical points
Winner, 3 Loser, 1	when the margin is 1 to 11 and the loser scored at least one technical point
Winner, 3 Loser, 0	when the margin is 1 to 11 and the loser scored no technical points

In elimination for passivity, the points awarded will be like this:

Winner, 3.5 Loser, 0	when there are 12 or more points difference between the wrestlers
Winner, 3 Loser, 0	if at the time of elimination the winner has scored less than 12 technical points
Winner, 2 Loser, 0	when the winner has scored no points

A second defeat in a round-robin competition does not bring elimination. The wrestlers still must wrestle the opponents they haven't yet met.

BYE

A BYE occurs when the odd wrestler moves on to the next round. The wrestler who's given a bye doesn't earn positive points. Neither does a wrestler who is disqualified for wrestling without action, passively, and with no points.

FINALS

The contestants that place in positions 1, 2, and 3 (in the elimination rounds of their pool) go on to the finals. Third place in each pool wrestle for fifth and sixth place; second place in each pool, for third and fourth; and first place in each pool vie for first and second place. These head-to-head bouts determine the final standings in each weight and age category.

TEAM SCORING

The top-two wrestlers in each age and weight category also may score team points for their team.

Here's the point system for team scores in AAU wrestling:

First place	10
Second	7
Third	5
Fourth	3
Fifth	2
Sixth	1

AFTERWORD

DIFFERENCES AMONG ASSOCIATIONS

As mentioned previously, the AAU wrestling uses a system of rules very similar to those of FILA, the governing body that regulates the rules used in the Olympics and monitors the sport world-wide. If you were to attend a high school or college wrestling event in the U.S., you'd be struck immediately by the superficial differences. The singlets are red and green rather than red and blue, high school wrestlers use ear protectors while others do not, the mats are somewhat larger with slightly different markings. The high school and college associations also have their own weight classes to fill, which are slightly different from one another, and obviously they don't need to worry about ten- or forty-year-olds participating in the sport.

As the bouts began you would notice other differences. From style to style, a few different holds are barred and the scoring and duties of the officials vary slightly. Takedowns are a little more dramatic in an AAU wrestling competition, and the coaches have a little more input during an NCAA bout.

One difference that is important to be aware of is that the NCAA employs the idea of time advantage, or "riding time," in their scoring system. The wrestler who achieves a takedown and proceeds to dominate the opponent may score further by maintaining control. The contestant with a sufficient margin of riding time is awarded an extra point. In AAU competition, it's likely the ref would simply stand up the participants (i.e., bring them back to the center of the mat) and restart the wrestling if one wrestler were riding another.

But whatever the small, particular differences, these styles are certainly spiritual brothers and they are involved with the same sport, just the way that Pony Leaguers and the New York Mets are both playing baseball.

To obtain a copy of the 1989 Amateur Athletic Union Wrestling Rules Manual, please enclose $8.00 check or money order made payable to: AAU Wrestling Rules Manual (U.S. funds only) and mail to:

1989 AAU Wrestling Rules Manual
P.O. Box 68207
Indianapolis, IN 46468

Your manual will be mailed first class and postage paid.

Name _____

Address _____

City _____

State _____ Zip _____